# NEVER A DAY GO BYE:
## *You Make Me Dream*

---

### ANDREW MARSHALL, JR.

Copyright © 2024 Andrew Marshall, Jr.

All rights reserved. No part of this book may be reproduced, stored, or transmitted by any means—whether auditory, graphic, mechanical, or electronic—without written permission of both publisher and author, except in the case of brief excerpts used in critical articles and reviews. Unauthorized reproduction of any part of this work is illegal and is punishable by law.

ISBN: 978-1-63950-253-0 (sc)
ISBN: 978-1-63950-254-7 (e)

This publication contains the opinions and ideas of its author. It is intended to provide helpful and informative material on the subjects addressed in the publication. The author and publisher specifically disclaim all responsibility for any liability, loss, or risk, personal or otherwise, which is incurred as a consequence, directly or indirectly, of the use and application of any of the contents of this book.

Writers Apex

Gateway Towards Success

8063 MADISON AVE #1252
Indianapolis, IN 46227
+13176596889
www.writersapex.com

*Dedicated to*
*LOVE TRUEST LOVERS*
*of THE LOVE....*

## Never A Day Go Bye: You Make Me Dream

I *dream* of dreams that are Dreaming of You;
There's Never a day that My Dream's Untrue.
A Life of Love For You Means EVERYTHING.
Only time can Tell if true LOVE *HATES Mean:*
Do tell LOVE rumblings are a last *earthquake.*
Tell Love You are Sincere: *love-made mistake!*
LOVE Lasts From Beginning to End of Dream.
Dreaming of love might make *A sleep scream!*
Where's the LAZY *Sun* who just wants to SIT?
Love's two-*breasted* LOVERs can Hide a TIT!
Whoever barters with Love makes SIDE BET?
Give Love Your Best Umbrella: Water *is WET!*
After The FIRE burns out, *LOVE-Grow-*DARK!
*LOVE* KNOWS 1 fury like 2 scorned HEARTS.

## ABOUT THE BOOK

This book is an attempt to *unswallow LOVE's swallowed tongue*.

### Love's Swallowed Tongue

Listen to love's truthful tongue!
Do you hear baby-bite-marks on love's fangs?
When love's blood never dries,
Does love pain leave death-devouring-stains?
Look into the mouth where love swallows its heart!
Do you see that love's wisdom teeth haven't wisely grown?
Love shall poke its tongue at the meddling road
That's much too narrow to be so-forking-long …

# Contents

## NEVER A DAY GO BYE

I Try Too Hard ................................................................... 2

The Bluebonnet's Flew (House Sparrows) ........................ 3

Never a Day Go Bye ......................................................... 4

Yo' Child? (Raised Hell Well) ........................................... 5

What's The Name of Your Song?
  (The Songs You Aren't Singing) ................................... 6

You are More Poor (Beautiful) Than Pure ....................... 7

Our Voices ........................................................................ 8

Time (or "Revelation") ..................................................... 9

A Drink Away from Sorrow ............................................ 10

A Taste for Love's Soul .................................................. 11

Strange to Me Too, Love ................................................ 12

The Presumptions for Love ............................................ 13

I Did Not Break Your Promise to Me ............................ 14

God Whispers ................................................................. 15

The Absence of Love ("Fly Free") ................................. 16

Only Once Dreamed Like My Dreamer ........................ 17

I Am So Melancholy ....................................................... 18

One Day's Respect .......................................................... 19

Magic Black .................................................................... 20

Truth ............................................................................... 21

Lie, But Don't Lie to Yourself (a "Slang" Love Song) ..... 22

| | |
|---|---|
| My Song | 23 |
| Bartering for Love's Rebate | 25 |
| Love's Little Liar Loves Lying | 26 |
| I Sing to the Heart of My Soul | 27 |
| Midnight Visitations | 28 |
| Non-Amour | 29 |
| Only Your Everlasting Love | 30 |
| Down the Up Climb | 31 |
| Drum Song | 32 |
| Break Free | 33 |
| Miss Love | 34 |
| Before Forever Go Astray | 35 |
| A Soul Mate for the Soakings of Summer | 36 |
| The Two Faces of a Tear (Across The Line) | 37 |
| Broke Spirit | 38 |
| The Mirror of Me (Underlying Eyes) | 39 |
| Love is Two Faced, Too | 40 |
| To My Mistress of Life | 41 |
| My Heart | 42 |
| They Keep Changing Upon The Colors | 43 |
| New-Moan-Ya' | 44 |
| Irritating Vows | 45 |
| Sticking Up | 46 |
| Missing My Feelings | 47 |
| If Not By None Other | 48 |
| Mankind Suffrage | 49 |
| Love's Swallowed Tongue | 50 |

# YOU MAKE ME DREAM

Weather Coming and Going For True Love ................................ 52
The Dreamer Must Not Sleep With The Dream ........................ 53
Love's Forgiven ............................................................................. 54
Long After Love Has Left And Still Refuses to Leave ................ 55
Until Love Begs To Moan (Imagining the Darkness in Night) ... 56
Dream's Limitation ........................................................................ 57
Darkness ......................................................................................... 58
Cry for Me in the Private of Your Privacy .................................. 59
So Blessed My Love's Not Fond of the First Stone ..................... 60
In My Dream's Dream (This Day) ............................................... 61
So! Freedom is Still The Slowest .................................................. 62
Lover of a Night Dream ................................................................ 63
Fantasy ............................................................................................ 64
Me and My Heart .......................................................................... 65
You Make Me Dream (Heaven's Loveliest Transition) ............... 66
My Love, My Dove
 ("Another Time") ....................................................................... 67
Do Not Take No Wish Away From The Wishful Night ............. 69
The Un-Lover of The Love ........................................................... 70
The Brink of Love .......................................................................... 72
As if Love Did Not Wave Back At The Magician's Wand ......... 73
Mama Babies (One Day) ............................................................... 74
However We Grin .......................................................................... 75
Coming Past the First Stop ........................................................... 76
The Midnight Walk ....................................................................... 77
I Wish I Were The Last Wish Granted to a Wish ....................... 78

Love!? You'd Better Leave Me Alone Now, Love
  (Love's Undertaker?) ................................................................ 79
Let Us Sing Our Own Songs of Love And Salvation ................ 80
Shady, Child ................................................................................ 81
Love Has Already Been Interrupted From Saying Goodnight ..... 82
One Missed Stop Alone ............................................................. 84
The Night is Not Shy ................................................................. 85
Hear the Mime Gesturing .......................................................... 86
Don't Like The Way You Left Me for Gone .............................. 87
Supper at Dawn .......................................................................... 88
We Taught Our Doubles How to Walk, Too ............................ 89
After The Days of Dark Love .................................................... 90
Any Weather (We Know'd That it Was Gonna Rain) ............... 91
My Heart Lied to Forget About You ......................................... 92
Wearing The Presents I Bring .................................................... 93
Save Me a Big Corner ................................................................ 94
One Light (Let's Just Say We Rode) ......................................... 95
Your Picture ................................................................................ 96
Get to Chasing My Dream ........................................................ 97
If My Love Couldn't Swim ........................................................ 98
Only Our Level of Love ............................................................. 99
Do Not Take Our Love to Love's Early Grave ........................ 100
A Split in Love's Hair ............................................................... 101
The Ultimate Love Loves Ultimately ...................................... 102

# NEVER A DAY GO BYE

# I Try Too Hard

I try too hard,
To cry so little.
Harder I TRY,
Tear BIGGER.

# The Bluebonnet's Flew (House Sparrows)

*LOVE,*
We did run out,
What about YOU?
"Y'all *kissers* won't see me again,
After *unbuckling MY flu-footed-shoe!*"

LOVE,
We all *underflowed*,
How *over-empty* is YOU?
"Spreading *transmissible* LOVE,
*Bruising wings* like *house sparrows do!*"

# Never a Day Go Bye

Never a Day Go Bye,
That I do not die,
True and unshy!
Never a Day Go Bye,
That I don't BEG:
LOVE, tell "*why!?*"

# Yo' Child?
## (Raised Hell Well)

If your *mama* did wreck the child,
Then who else rear-ended YOU?
Yo' child?
If love can be Shamed or Tamed,
Then why isn't YOUR love TRUE?
Yo' child?
Don't get up there telling on Love's
MOTHER; she couldn't have done
Any MORE than a MAMA WOULD.
What more can heaven need when
The *hell-raised* kill LOVE so GOOD?
Do the children want a lifetime deal?
"Why do one love hurt and bleed and
The other seem to never have a *feel*?
Yo' Child!

# What's The Name of Your Song?
# (The Songs You Aren't Singing)

What's The Name of Your Song?
Let me sing unto *You* until our chorus sounds alarms!
What's The Name of Your Song?
Is there a difference between love's hymns or harms?

## You are More Poor (Beautiful) Than Pure

You are also Uglier Than Sin!
(I believe this is what makes all my love grin.)
You're still just the prettier Sin!
(But from where else should *BEAUTY* begin?)

# Our Voices

You want me for my voice,
Singing the *SWEET* lullaby,
Begging the *die* for its love.
You want my voices to defy:
Carry love through its *voice*,
While the Voices *did* rejoice.

## Time (or "Revelation")

My life is not a secret,
Even with doubt unto itself.
If I could live life forever,
Time would still take my last breath.
Time and I,
Or, rather me against the beckoning wind,
Until the time that I am crossed over,
Living just now begins, again.
Oh!?
Time must continually be revolving,
Around that windless bend.
If I had the patience of time,
I'd steal away some time to *shoot*,
And have a shot of that clandestine *"SIN."*

# A Drink Away from Sorrow

I did not thirst for light-gold *Cristal*,
Just to settle for cheap filtered gin.
I command the crown of the shelf,
Cause the bottom has a deep end.

# A Taste for Love's Soul

Want to taste love's soul.
I want to know what love
Knows. I want to mix for
Ever and a salivated kiss.
I want a point-blank shot
At Love that cannot miss.

## Strange to Me Too, Love

You are strange to me,
And I've lived beyond
Love's expected eternity.
Love's not a pre-written,
Non-fictional-like novela.
Never is the facts fiction.
Love isn't unlike its death,
After living with *a* addiction….

# The Presumptions for Love

When love is tardy,
My whole disposition is absent.
Where I used to exemplify a
Love directing its Niceties,
I may choose to be naughty.
Don't leave your love light on,
Not for endarkened Me.
I can always find a love,
Blind as a dark skinned,
Light-headed, bat,
And fly away, far,
Feeling like I'm accepted
As one of the *dearly beloved,*
*Imprisoned, yet Freed.*

## I Did Not Break Your Promise to Me

You said, "Love cannot be captured,
Unless it is free."
Tell my heart who is the wise.
Is there anything about true love that love won't disguise?
What if love broke the heart of God?
Like that time when sin was honored, not despised.
But, I did not break *Love's* promise to me.

## God Whispers

Lord,
Whisper innocently into my barren heart.
Stick like that gluey substandard.
Then, let's bond in promise to never depart.
Show me the difference 'tween night,
And a day gone terribly wrong.
If I am going to go,
Why aren't the freedom killers gone?
If they are destined to stay,
Then why look back?
If heaven paves her streets in gold,
Why is hell Illuminated in the darkness of
It's darkest *Black*?

# The Absence of Love ("Fly Free")

When love is absent
My whole world is tardy.
Where I used to respect
Love's niceties,
The *Lover* chose to chase its
*NAUGHTY!*
Don't leave your love light on,
Not for dis-enlightened me,
I'm off to love a lover,
Blind as this "dungy" (vs."dingy") *Bat*,
AND, *Fly-Open-Free.*

## Only Once Dreamed Like My Dreamer

In this COLD world,
I'm tempted to step
Outside the Inferno.
Dream ME heavens
That can melt Snow.
In that same Dream,
Heaven melting Hell,
I know this was *YOU*,
But can't really *TELL*.

# I Am So Melancholy

My soul has melted *MY Heart*.
Given the way feelings do feel,
Got off to My much better start.
I am just as unhappy as a heel
Beginning the *sorrowfully* march.

## One Day's Respect

One day, you did swear,
That you loved me.
Next day, love is running late.
If loving were a job,
You would be demoted,
To not opening heaven's gate.
One day, you made the promise that
"Love will never leave!"
Before the sun could set….
Just know "My heart is not pleased!"
If love must take any more
Than my heart should not give,
I beg only of love –
To one day respect the way love makes love feel.

## Magic Black

How do you always come shining through?
Is it the lackeration of MELANIN w/o HUE?
Then, why isn't the FOOL Destiny-in-view?
ALL do live and die to see life in *REVIEW*?

# Truth

Truth is like love,
Painful, and mostly - elusive.
Truth will not remain mysteriously possessed,
Nor does Truth make disingenuous embrace.
Truth is the ultimate, uninhibited ecstasy,
A sensual, unabated foreplay,
The anticipation of who is *becoming*.
Like Creation's loveliest gifts.
The *Truth* is not *unlike the Truest Love*.

# Lie, But Don't Lie to Yourself
## (a "Slang" Love Song)

Have you ever tested time?
When she stopped speaking, did she rhyme?
And your love moves my finger away from the clock,
Didn't your heartbeat flutter, had time not stop?
I'll give you more life than you could take back.
With your need to be filled up,
You cannot withstand that?
Lie, but don't lie to yourself;
You even love the sex in my breath.
And before the world comes to its end,
You'll want to die believing you could relive it again.
And this time, I am the thief in theft.
I was the best you never laid down with,
Just to move on over and *fake* your rest.

# My Song

You are taking me back now,
That used to be my groove.
Young cats today don't know about
The steps that must be taken to visit "Old School."
We learned to take the noise outside,
Inside the home, our mamas didn't play.
Except for time wasted promoting procreation,
During the plight, life didn't seem worth living,
Back in the heyday.
I do recall popping my fingers
To my crush's syncopated beat.
And don't talk about my dancing,
Couldn't un-coordinate neither right feet.
Everybody loved one another,
Swore never to find a reason to cheat!
Reminiscing isn't about the shades of blues black comes in,
That would negatively impact the nostalgia of a memory too sweet.
It's not only about their way of life that made me green,
Or how to live and be alive, simultaneously, is plain mean,
It is a necessity for the chorus to join in on your song,
And pray that another sugary-talking lover come singing along.

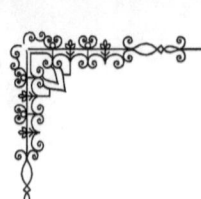

But, the former will always be my song!
That past is the hands of my God diverting me through harm.
The spirit of my ancestors who dared to awake in their alarm.
This, and infinitely more, compose the melodies in my song,
For as long as I might not forever again so live.
Only heaven knows that anytime is the right time for reminiscing,
And that a defunct life could have some other than morbid appeal.

echo:
There is something
That will always be my song,
Until the day that I shall again live.
I don't know why I lived to reminisce,
Or why a dying love has such appeal.

# Bartering for Love's Rebate

I will give you love that I have missed.
We shall look to forever,
Where there is no end to a lovely kiss.

I will give you a love that cannot die.
Travel to your farthest dreams,
Then abolish any limit placed on the sky.

I will dry your tears before they do cry.
Then reveal to love's epiphany
That honest love does not lie.

Walking hand in hands through the pearly gates,
We shall outlive eternity,
And give heaven back a love rebate.

# Love's Little Liar Loves Lying

Yes....
I did *imply* that I *would*
Always love you.
But...
*You've* lied to *ourselves*,
Too!

# I Sing to the Heart of My Soul

I sing the melodies of my song only to you,
So that the doves do know my love is true.
When heaven should rebuild her castle,
The first of love's last rocks of stone,
Shall be cast to baptize love anew.
Let me cleanse my soul from impurities,
And drown in love's highest reveal of perfection,
Like a virgin who will not hesitate to give it up to
Life's first bought lessons.

## Midnight Visitations

"I'm coming back home now,
Reason being, there is nothing.
Been milling and billing,
In other words, saving souls in the names of everyone else.
Since life placed chains and shackles on you,
Heaven knows you are on your own.
Guess you must not burden salvation,
Until after forever has truly waited too long, and is now gone.
Given your pleas to be delivered from evil,
Praying isn't like an immaculate, gentile cure.
Just wanted to lift your spirits up,
But that direction is darkened for the tainted pure.
So, let's take it back to the beginning,
Before life made you wander away
And then submit to temptation's willingness.
Do know that Death does not reward
with retroactive compensation,
For the services that were rendered in your dead years."

## Non-Amour

Love works harder as the days are shortened to too long,
And still searches for love during the soft of the night.
Not that love is blind to discerning near perfection,
But that love cannot afford to excuse its inner sight.
A few smaller infractions of harmless misdemeanors,
Can escalate to a criminalizing best.
With respect to inciting emotions,
Love, then, shall always fail the heart's
More unforgiving test.

## Only Your Everlasting Love

Only the everlasting love
Shall never set its heart free.
The heart is its wayward soul,
Despite the conflict in *THEE*.
There are some pains that, if,
Only love could console,
May lead the dreamer to dream love-like-BOLD.
Whether loving blindly, blinded by LOVE,
Or, in YOUR own unsighted-ness, just can't see,
Make YOUR own everlasting LOVE that
NEVER quit loving after the heart's been so *FREE*....

## Down the Up Climb

We who cannot get up the hill,
Must continue a vertical climb,
Only to arrive and then forgive.

# Drum Song

My heart beats for your undaunting Love,
Pounding with the drums of heaven above.
The lifeline that flows wine into love's vine.
The melodic beauty that perfects with time.
The truth that none wiser has never known.
The reception of forever that we're our own.

# Break Free

Let me be the love to you
That you are to me.
Let's let us be *imprisoned*
As love breaks free.

## Miss Love

Some stiffs still owe you!
Uneven is the score, too.
Jazzy loins dig and swell,
Kissed by lovely *Jezebel*.

# Before Forever Go Astray

One day with you is a lifetime away.
Shall yesterday bequeath tomorrow,
Before forever dies and goes astray?

## A Soul Mate for the Soakings of Summer

Sometimes you make this
*WINTERED* Soul believe
Love's a *SPRING* to *FALL*.

# The Two Faces of a Tear
## (Across The Line)

Cross that line with me,
And We shall finish together!
The line is drawn to separate
The withering of the *Bird's* feathers.

Cross your heart with me;
You are the lead-vote-getter!
*Lying* separates a two-faced-tear,
Though both lies is equally *wetter*.

## Broke Spirit

Death cannot break love's spirit,
Although *dead* is the life breaker.
None but the dead do not fear it:
Love is not the *dying* Undertaker

# The Mirror of Me
## (Underlying Eyes)

Look into my eyes and tell me that you
Do ever love me.
Tell me that my eyes could never lie to
Love's heavenly.
Tell me what I would tell you if I were to
Tell love to *belie*.
Look into my eyes and tell me that you
Love who you see.
Tell me that my eyes could never lie to
*MY* mirror of *ME*.

# Love is Two Faced, Too

Who doesn't love Love,
Or who don't Love love?
Love is not too uncaring,
Love doesn't like sharing.

## To My Mistress of Life

You do know that after you refused to leave,
I did grow a bit unusually dependent,
Crazy-headed, and a foolish pride-like.
At one point in time,
Didn't even help myself.
Just couldn't bear the taste no more,
of that forbearing love, for no longer.
And each time when you do come back home, finding me,
I am always consoled by a pain that welcomes itself to stay over,
and don't leave, long after you should have never been so long gone.

# My Heart

Embellish my love, within you,
My loveliest,
And I will not ridicule my blushing pride.
Send me your most extraordinary - beautiful, and true,
And I will not make my fears run or hide,
After stealing a kiss from intoxicating lips,
Whose innocence is an immaculate pure.
That heaven lives inside your heart,
Of this, My love has made me sure.
Make my truth speak with a tongue,
That you know is liar proof,
If eternity is our sight unlimited,
Then forever will be our love's abiding roof.
To this togetherness that our souls did commend,
I submit to you from my only lasting heart:
We are now the perfect picture of the Master's peace,
And nothing can ever tear our canvases apart.

## They Keep Changing Upon The Colors

You don't succumb to anybody,
Just because they love the Hue.
To tell a good lie, I don't want to
Be the one who looks like YOU.
You are now the lighter BLACK,
While I am its DARKEST BLUE.
*WE damned!* US *chameleon #2.*

# New-Moan-Ya'

The walking-N kinds.
Not keeping its finds.
The Cold chases the
Running in the Rains,
Spitting up the Bloods
Of Your History *Stains*.

## *Irritating Vows*

Bowels are irritated,
Because of Y-O-U!
Always making me -
"DO!" "DO!"

## Sticking Up

Love has its limitations,
But hate is endless too.
Point *none* a sour finger,
Like the *Middle* wants to.

# Missing My Feelings

How do your feelings do feel?
Do they feel the ill of the feel?
Want to feel the feeling's feel!
Can look up climbing downhill.

## If Not By None Other

Save me, Love,
And I shall repent.
Hell was not fornicated
By birthing an accident.

Save me Love,
And salivate the soul.
On the road back to
My Motherlode.

Save me Love,
And deliver back to Mother,
To whom I am truly loved,
If not by none other.

# Mankind Suffrage

Why do you make your woman suffer,
When you need her to run your race?
Hate only silence like a *muted muffler*,
Without thy woman love has no trace!

## Love's Swallowed Tongue

Listen to love's truthful tongue!
Do you *hear* baby-bite-marks on love's fangs?
When love's blood never dries,
Does love pain leave death-devouring-stains?
Look into the mouth where love swallows its heart!
Do you see that love's wisdom teeth haven't wisely grown?
Love shall poke its tongue at the meddling road
That's much too narrow to be *so-forking-long* ….

# YOU MAKE ME DREAM

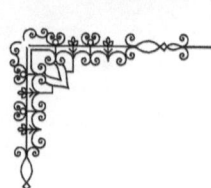

# Weather Coming and Going For True Love

*LOVE* KNOWS 1 fury like 2 scorned HEARTS.
After The FIRE burns out, *LOVE Grow* DARK:
Give Love Your Best Umbrella: *Water'S WET!*
Whoever barters with Love makes SIDE BET?
Love's two-*breasted* LOVERs can Hide a TIT!
Where's the LAZY *Sun* who just wants to SIT?
Dreaming of love might make *A sleep scream!*
LOVE Lasts From Beginning to End of Dream.
Tell Love You are Sincere: *love-made mistake!*
Do tell LOVE rumblings are a last *earthquake.*
Only time can Tell if true LOVE *HATES* Mean.
A Life of Love For You Means EVERYTHING.
There's Never a day that My Dream's Untrue.
I *Dream* of Dreams That are Dreaming of You.

# The Dreamer Must Not Sleep With The Dream

Sell me one of love's honest DREAMS.
And let imagination become MY EYES.
A DREAM shall always live to DREAM,
UNTIL the Dreamer *SLEEPS* and *DIES*.

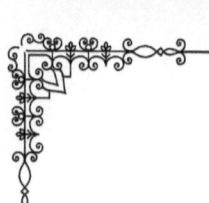

## Love's Forgiven

Love has *no-unforgivable-sin*,
Love losers *always-didn't-win*.
Love isn't connected, together,
At the upper, inside *of-lust-HIP*.
So, it might not *have-been-love*
That slipped thru *a-heaven-grip*....

## Long After Love Has Left And Still Refuses to Leave

So….I still love only talking to my no less loveable,
More liquid-fied, love being loquacious,
And answering back to love, MYSELF….
*LOVE's EVERLASTING LOVE IS BLIND-NOT-DEAF!*
Anybody can see that LOVE does not always leave,
LONG AFTER LIFE HAS PACKED ITS HEART,
AND, DONE, LEFT….

# Until Love Begs To Moan
## (Imagining the Darkness in Night)

I will do nothing lower,
(other than some more of *this*....)
I will kiss your soreness slower,
(if it's love's *orgasmatic* wish....)
So that WE do not misunderstand,
Let's both take the other by EACH hand!?
Make LOVE feel like love's TOO GROWN!
*Give* a KISS and make LOVE *beg* its MOAN....

## Dream's Limitation

Do you create dream's limitation,
Or dare make a dreamer expand?
How long can a dream keep *living*,
Until dying *before* dreaming again?

# Darkness

Shut this life's revolving door;
Don't wish to see no sunshine.
Can't weather the pain no more;
Heat's frozen love's heart in time.

# Cry for Me in the Private of Your Privacy

Cry for me in the hollow of your own privacy.
Let's become orgasm-seeking, fool-less free.
We will have the calm of the falsifying climax,
Memories full of "Adult-Pornagraphic-Estacy."

## So Blessed My Love's Not Fond of the First Stone

The distances between here and there were
The same times travelled from then and now.
Time and distance is like a relative who came
Just to eat, but ends up tearing down a *House*.

# In My Dream's Dream (This Day)

I dreamed that you came back for me.
I dreamed that *This Day* I'd get to see.
I dreamed of the dreams of my dream.
Can't let darkness hear *A dream scream*.

# So! Freedom is Still The Slowest

Slow death and fast snail
Entered a race.
Slow death lost,
Cause of the snail's pace.

*Contest-a-ment:*

Want my *footsteps* traced!
"Death doesn't lose its race,
(nor does Hell repent)"

# Lover of a Night Dream

My Night Dreamer lures me to *The Sleep*,
Prays for me that my *weeper-won't-weep*.
Charges *freedom* for any payment to love,
Hearts are *One Soul*, ascending to *Above*.

# Fantasy

If you cannot fantasize,
Then dreaming is not wise.
A dream is worthy of dreaming
When your fantasies can be realized.
A fantasy is just a dream
With an element of surprise.
A dream loves fantasies,
Wherever they do refuse to compromise.
Your dreams can be so awesomely cool,
While your fantasies might dislike heat.
If your dreams should die in a fatal sleep,
Then your fantasies can't wake and weep.
If you cannot dream of a fantasy,
Fantasy's dreams will not survive.
You could live without the hope of ever day-dreaming,
But fantasizing keeps your dark days from dying, *SO ALIVE*.

# Me and My Heart

Me and my heart shall never grow apart.
Shall never lose its grip,
nor be sunken by a *loose* lip.

Me and my heart shall never fail to befriend,
The love that can make us grin,
or the mirror that looks at *us* from outwardly-in.

Me and my heart *struggles* at replacing broken pieces,
But me and my heart shall love and live and lie
like sleeping souls during a mating of seasons.

## You Make Me Dream
## (Heaven's Loveliest Transition)

I died waiting to love *LOVE* again,
And I awakened a love that's true.
I want to love the ways of a friend,
Dying to give the love back to you!
Want to begin with love once again,
The ways heaven sleep and *re-new*.

# My Love, My Dove
## ("Another Time")

I saw my precipitating death's *Afterlife*,
And all the ones I loved,
Loved me, along with all of
The others whose life they did flee:
My Love! The Dove! Come back for Me.
Make the souls rest far away from
This arrested unrestedness that
Only with death dying might set love up for a freedom.
But death never dies! I know
From the dying love, inside my heart, still chasing after ME.
I will trade you my next life for
The last life with My Love! The Dove! (No swindles!)
What life can make its time back up,
Sliding down this winding, upwardly *morbid* hill?
"Only My Love! The Dove!"
My Love! The Dove!
Can take me places where even a dying heart,
Before eminent death, gets hit softly with Death's death blow?

To know death, all you have to do is:
"Get You a sampled taste of this life,
Without having acquiesced to *Love's-Tenderest-Temptations*."
Never knew that loveliness can almost truly die
To know so much less about *The Dove*.
Losing time to chastise time isn't being time sensitive. Maybe,
*Un-timeless, time-consuming, missed-its-timing,
Misfortune of time.*
Because *TIME* set its own *TIME*, too!
Too painfully fast, *AND*,
Or, *BOTH*, too posthumously slow....

# Do Not Take No Wish Away From The Wishful Night

The night has travelled from sea to sea,
Encircling the moon and unwritten, free.
The night has hitch-hiked with lazy grey,
Along the trails where dreams do *replay*.

# The Un-Lover of The Love

Love's revenge is a unloving
Hate for Love,
Before and After Love.
For the love of hated love,
Unlove your hate for Love,
Go love your hate for Love,
But neither hate the Lover of Love!
So, Love propose, again, that
Love Exonerate Love's
Un-Lover of The Love.
Purposely, un-loved-un-proposed,
As if a dove was left,
In the Road, un-killed,
Or love's unloved had been willed
To love's *Full Bounty*,
Heart attacking Love's lovelessness:
Love's hope when casting
Love's Lover Lure was that
The heart give a pitiful willingly,
Albeit through the un-magically,
Propose to depose love's deposition.
But What is, Remains, or, Maybe,
Already wasn't going to know love's
Forever, while one Love and the other Love
Never could get both *Loves* together.
Let Love come crawling to rub

A all loved-up (un-maximized thumping) head,
Love would see its Love's Grin,
*Or, A Love Have Been Again,*
*After locking out love so lovelessly,*
*Where only Love could let Love back in.*
Let love not love with its hate for love.
Too much lesser Love become,
When The Un-Lover of Love isn't
Love's *Loveliest of all Love's Lovely Loved Ones*….

# The Brink of Love

Bring me back from the brink of my years,
Let love remove all fear of my lasting tears.
Bring me to love, when *Love* pay attention,
Where the brink of love is paid *no mention*.

# As if Love Did Not Wave Back At The Magician's Wand

I can, too, make Love Disappear!
I can do bad trick and love hears!

## Mama Babies (One Day)

I'm gonna forever be your *only* child,
And wish to never go breaking away.
Make me come back home someday.
Do I *suckle* the nipple down to the dream's womb?
When might heaven remarry the bride and groom?
My mama do still sing ME deep-belly,
Burning, dreamy, rhythm and blue-sy,
Keep on screaming until you can hear
Yourself songs, wearing her veil that's
Too long for its own reach. Give me the
Song to sing to OUR children, but YOU
Give them their heart beat. *LOOKS* are
Long and Wide that OUR LOVE sweep.
Life-food for all who do eat. Does life die
When living its lie? Take me to that next
*Garden* where none wish to return. Can
You take me when Love starts to BURN?
But if you should take me back to THEN,
When I was to live-like and walk with God
A *Certain* way, do I still get to come back
Home...*One Day?*

## However We Grin

I would have fallen, too,
Had I not caught Myself.
Love throws a first stone,
Loving to dust what's left.

## Coming Past the First Stop

Past the First Evolution,
Turn Love loose...
*LITTLE* train is less *One*
Lover,
*The CABOOSE.*

## The Midnight Walk

As soon as WE *stand* up,
You want to start THE *back talking*.
But DEATH stretches for
It's LONELY MIGRATION,
Before running into a dark Midnight,
*WALKING….*

# I Wish I Were The Last Wish Granted to a Wish

I wish I were not the envy for wishing.
I wish I were a less truer premonition.
I wish I were a wisher for the wishers,
I'd wish for Love full of kissing kissers.

# Love!? You'd Better Leave Me Alone Now, Love (Love's Undertaker?)

Leave me alone now, Love!
I'm done, done told you now.
Cannot make love love *back*,
Anyhow?

Leave me alone now, Love!
Too much pain for the GAIN!
I'm done, DONE telling love,
No Shame!

Leave me alone now, Love!
Besides, I am already *taken*.
*Past time*, my love didn't die,
MISTAKEN?

# Let Us Sing Our Own Songs of Love And Salvation

Our Voices must sing the *song of love connotation*.
But give them peace during their love hibernations.
Our Voices must sound the trumpet for One Nation.
Let Us Sing Our Own Songs of Love And Salvation.

## Shady, Child

The shaded child sees life from eyes heavily closed. Life DROWN from flood Water runnin' down on *Who KNOWS!*

# Love Has Already Been Interrupted From Saying Goodnight

Love said,
"We'd better be getting OUR *Gone* on!?":
Arrivederci and,
SO? LONG!
Learn from US,
OUR life longest….
FRIEND?
Together, Let's not WASTE
THIS LOVE
Awaiting another lost chance
Just to do it AGAIN.
For when WE do,
*US* shall know
ONE language so
DIRE,
Sticks like OPENER
To the CLOSED eye.
Life is saying,
SAYONARA,
BON VOYAGE,

AND TO THE TRUE HUE,
SOUTHERN NEIGHBORS,
"SAWUBONA!"
USE YOUR heads *HOOD*,
*Re-Languish UP* (suppose to be "Language")
REMOVE FROM-THEE-THY HATER,
THEN, YOU MAY TELL "ALL":
"Bye Bye"
Will bite the snakes, a Lil' Bit' *"LATER!"*
WE *fin* to be GONE!
*KNEES-KNOTTED*,
PRAYING FOR US,
Cause *it's* NEVER
Gonna get to be but *SO LONG*…..

## One Missed Stop Alone

I walk along with Alone,
Following northern star,
Falling, southern bound.
The Star's the LOWERS
Love UPPER MOBILITY.
Whereabout do WE Find
OUR light year Cometh?.
The Northern Star betting
On crop of Hope baggers,
Still brings forth a *YIELD*!.

# The Night is Not Shy

The night is not shy,
And *here* being why:
The night sees plenty
With the specked-eye;
A steady streak of *un-*
*Stroked* Luck don't lie.

## Hear the Mime Gesturing

How many hours invade
Just one minute?
If love is sealed in stone,
Only love's in it?
Many days go uncovered,
In the life running
Out of its own TIME.
The ways that life performs,
Personifies *MINE*.

# Don't Like The Way You Left Me for Gone

I wasn't done,
But did not know,
That you were simmering
So awfully slow…
Didn't know this:
Love cares more about
Who's first to stop
Giving out love,
No MORE!

# Supper at Dawn

Inspect tonight,
For in the morning,
A calm to the *Trust*.
The speck in Your eye
Is another remnant of *US*.
But the tears in the memories
Cannot be dried like blood
That has caked too long.
The specks in those eyes are
Seen from twisted lens,
Unfocused on it's wrongs.

# We Taught Our Doubles How to Walk, Too

Why do you wear but One shoe?
Cause I was trying to give THEM
Both a walk on the backs of YOU:
Wants US to wear one in the front,
And another one in the back, TOO.
You may wear each strutting-LIKE,
Or be *worn* on the collar, *My Shoe*.

## After The Days of Dark Love

Forty days of darkness,
NO thanks to Our blues.
But the *colder* the days,
More *SUNSHINE* Rules.

# Any Weather (We Know'd That it Was Gonna Rain)

Walk in love with ME,
And love's walk's true.
Forever we shall walk
Like old *WALKER*s Do.

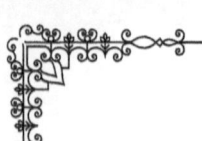

# My Heart Lied to Forget About You

Love never dies, but is Alive.
And forgetfulness gets harder,
The harder loving plenty tries.
I tried an easy remembrance,
But remembering is too easy,
After kissing heaven *goodbye*.

# Wearing The Presents I Bring

A cheap bottle of water to thirst
A white liver like, hydrated high,
To make death just as well-sick.
Stick a *needed* love in my arms.
My heart melts for frozen warm.
Let's just be disagreeable on one
Less of the endless list of things:
When arriving at Your FUNERAL-
WEDDING, You will always wear
The only present *YOU* must bring.

## Save Me a Big Corner

We have to do it on Gin
Not that *cheapen* bottle,
Taking you from US SIN.
And not that stuff makin'
You drunk with kindness.
Respecting a HangOver,
Only the lightning BEST!
*See*, Up shall look Down.
All of heaven's hellraisers
Are from *The Undertown*.
Some wear shy like bold.
No cares that once young
Isn't looking to see its old.
Many reasons for washout:
Sleep flooding My Dreams.
I feel the spirit, death need
Not to come back to Preach,
While death gives bottles of
Broken sleep an easy reach.

# One Light
## (Let's Just Say We Rode)

Let us stretch love's love beyond love's horizon,
    Out distancing less visionary eyes.
Let us love with one heart that's none surprising,
    Love's light's the transparent guide.
Let us carry one light dancing *the envying strode*.
    Let's ride forever and say *WE rode*.

# Your Picture

Your pictures shall be Re-taken,
So give them looks that outlasts
Those frozen in love's own time.
The camera's smile in your faces
Was the last for mysterious clues
That the eyes of the camera can't
Picture *dying-lying-winking-Blues*…..

# Get to Chasing My Dream

You are chasing my dreams,
Because my dreams are not dead.
You are chasing my dreams,
When dreaming is in one's *HEAD*.

You are chasing my dreams,
While my dreams are chasing, too.
But if you must be chasing my dream,
Chase my dream that catches *YOU*.

## If My Love Couldn't Swim

If my love could swim,
It would drown saving
My Love as love Floats.

If my love could *Swim*,
Forever I will *sail* YOU
Love's *unsinkable* boat.

# Only Our Level of Love

Look at Me at OUR eyes level,
No peeking,
But attempting to find *THE* heart.
Strip search truth,
Before love gets too dark.
Then *await* for Me
At the midsection,
Where heaven kisses forever.
I will have already waited far too long (long enough),
Unless *WE* are truly on *this* level.

# Do Not Take Our Love to Love's Early Grave

DO NOT take YOUR Love to Love's Graves;
NO points for LOVE have ever been *Shaved*!
DO NOT take YOUR Love to Love's Graves;
Until ALL hearts repent Love can't be Saved!

# A Split in Love's Hair

Love charges the same price for *LOVE*
That love make believe was *Love-Free*.
Love is not just a blinded, bluffing dove,
Love with open eyes cannot always see.
Love finds love that *doxy rather* not keep.
Love's *insomniacs* do never get *no* sleep…

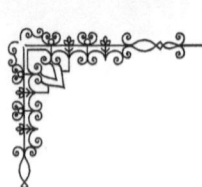

# *The Ultimate Love Loves Ultimately*

("Never a day go bye:YOU make ME dream")

Never A Day Go Bye! You make me DREAM!
Never A Day Go Bye! You make me DREAM!
Never A Day Go Bye! You make me DREAM!
Never A Day Go Bye! You make me DREAM!
Never A Day Go Bye! You make me DREAM!
Never A Day Go Bye! You make me DREAM!
Never A Day Go Bye! You make me DREAM!
Never A Day Go Bye! You make me DREAM!
Never A Day Go Bye! You make me DREAM!
Never A Day Go Bye! You make me DREAM!
Never A Day Go Bye! You make me DREAM!
Never A Day Go Bye! You make me DREAM!
Never A Day Go Bye! You make me DREAM!
Never A Day Go Bye! You make me DREAM!

Never A Day Go Bye! You make me DREAM!
Never A Day Go *Buy*…You *make* me DREAM….

www.ingramcontent.com/pod-product-compliance
Lightning Source LLC
Chambersburg PA
CBHW030556080526
44585CB00012B/398